AI-Powered SEO

Leveraging Zero-Click and E-E-A-T to Future-Proof Your Digital Strategy

Book Description:

As Artificial Intelligence continues to revolutionize industries worldwide, it's also reshaping the SEO landscape. In the era of AI-powered algorithms, **Zero-Click Searches** and **E-E-A-T** (Experience, Expertise, Authority, Trust) have become more crucial than ever for achieving online success. But how do you navigate this new frontier and ensure your SEO strategies are future-proof?

AI-Powered SEO takes an in-depth look at how **AI** is transforming SEO and how you can leverage **Zero-Click Searches** and **E-E-A-T** to stay ahead of the curve. This book provides actionable strategies for integrating AI-driven tools and content optimization tactics with Google's evolving ranking factors.

Here's what you'll learn:

- **AI and SEO Synergy**: Understand how AI tools can analyze search intent, optimize for **Zero-Click Searches**, and enhance content quality in line with **E-E-A-T** standards.
- **Mastering Zero-Click Searches with AI**: Discover how AI can help you rank in featured snippets, knowledge graphs, and other Zero-Click features by automating content creation, structured data, and search query analysis.
- **Building Content for E-E-A-T with AI**: How to use AI to create high-quality, authoritative content that meets Google's **E-E-A-T** criteria, from showcasing your experience to demonstrating trustworthiness.
- **AI-Driven Analytics for SEO**: Learn how AI-powered analytics tools can help track your SEO performance, adapt to algorithm changes, and predict trends in **Zero-Click Searches** and **E-E-A-T**.
- **Future-Proofing Your SEO Strategy**: Understand how AI will continue to impact SEO and how you can future-proof your digital strategy to stay competitive.

By combining AI insights with **Zero-Click Search** optimization and **E-E-A-T** best practices, *AI-Powered SEO* shows you how to drive more traffic, build stronger authority, and achieve long-term SEO success in a rapidly changing digital world.

CONTENTS:

- **Practical Strategies** for optimizing content to dominate Zero-Click Searches, including content structuring, schema markup, and answering user queries concisely.
- **Case Studies**: Examples of businesses successfully optimizing for Zero-Click Searches with AI-driven strategies.

Chapter 3: E-E-A-T – Building Trust in an AI-Driven World

- **What is E-E-A-T (Experience, Expertise, Authority, Trust)?**: A deep dive into Google's E-E-A-T ranking criteria.
- **AI's Role in E-E-A-T Optimization**: How AI tools can help build high-quality, authoritative content that demonstrates your experience and expertise.
- **Creating Content that Meets E-E-A-T**: Step-by-step guide on producing content that showcases authority, trustworthiness, and experience, using AI as a key tool.
- **How AI Helps Establish Trust**: Leveraging AI to analyze user behavior and improve trust signals on your website (reviews, testimonials, credible sources).

Chapter 4: Combining AI with Zero-Click Optimization for Maximum Impact

- **Merging AI with Zero-Click**: How to align AI-powered content creation with Zero-Click Search strategies.
- **AI Tools for Enhanced Zero-Click Optimization**: How tools like GPT-3 and

natural language processing (NLP) can automate content creation to fit Zero-Click formats.

- **Structured Data and Schema Markup**: Using AI to automatically generate structured data and schema for better visibility in Google's rich snippets.
- **Real-Life Examples**: Successful Zero-Click optimizations that leveraged AI-driven content.

Chapter 5: AI-Driven Analytics – Measuring Your SEO Success

- **AI-Powered Analytics**: How to use AI to track and analyze SEO performance, user behavior, and ranking trends.
- **Optimizing Your Strategy in Real-Time**: How AI analytics can provide insights into search intent, keyword optimization, and competitive analysis.
- **Predictive Analytics**: Using AI to predict SEO trends, helping you stay ahead of algorithm updates and shifts in search behavior.
- **Tools and Resources**: Recommended AI-powered SEO and analytics tools for measuring success and refining strategy.

Chapter 6: The Future of SEO – Adapting to AI and Search Algorithm Changes

- **How AI Will Continue to Shape SEO**: Exploring emerging trends in AI, voice search, machine learning, and how they'll affect SEO strategies.

- **The Role of Zero-Click and E-E-A-T in the Future of SEO**: Predictions for the continued relevance of Zero-Click and E-E-A-T, and how to future-proof your content.
- **Adapting to Algorithm Changes**: How AI will help you quickly adjust your SEO strategies in response to future Google algorithm updates.
- **Preparing for the Long-Term**: Preparing your digital strategy to thrive in an AI-driven SEO future.

Chapter 7: Actionable AI SEO Strategy for Long-Term Success

- **Building Your AI SEO Plan**: How to create a cohesive, long-term strategy using AI for Zero-Click and E-E-A-T optimization.
- **Key Steps to Take Today**: Actionable recommendations for businesses, marketers, and content creators to implement AI-powered SEO strategies immediately.
- **Tools and Resources**: A roundup of essential AI-driven tools for SEO, content creation, and performance tracking.
- **Creating a Sustainable SEO System**: How to continuously optimize and adjust your strategy for consistent, long-term growth.

Conclusion: Becoming an AI-Powered SEO Expert

- Recap of key concepts: **Zero-Click Searches**, **E-E-A-T**, and **AI-driven SEO**.
- Final thoughts on the future of SEO and AI's ongoing role in shaping digital strategies.
- How mastering AI-powered SEO will position you as a leader in the evolving SEO space.

Appendix: Resources for AI and SEO Tools

- A curated list of AI-powered SEO tools, analytics platforms, and content creation tools to help readers implement the strategies covered in the book.

This outline positions the book as a detailed, actionable guide that combines **AI**, **Zero-Click Search optimization**, and **E-E-A-T** principles to help you as businesses and content creators stay ahead in the rapidly changing SEO landscape. By focusing on these key concepts, the book offers practical insights and real-world strategies to succeed in both the present and future of SEO.

AI-Powered SEO

Leveraging Zero-Click and E-E-A-T to Future-Proof Your Digital Strategy

Introduction: The AI Revolution in SEO

The Transformative Role of AI in Modern SEO Practices

The digital landscape is evolving rapidly, and search engine optimization (SEO) is no exception. Artificial intelligence (AI) is at the forefront of this transformation, reshaping how search engines rank content and how users interact with information. Traditional SEO methods that once relied solely on keywords and backlinks are no longer sufficient. AI-powered algorithms now prioritize user intent, content quality, and engagement metrics, making it essential for marketers and content creators to adapt.

From Google's RankBrain to AI-generated content optimization tools, AI is revolutionizing SEO in unprecedented ways. It enhances search personalization, predicts user behavior, and refines content recommendations. Businesses that harness AI-driven strategies will gain a competitive edge, while those resistant to change risk becoming obsolete.

The Importance of Zero-Click Searches and E-E-A-T in the AI-Driven SEO Landscape

One of the most significant changes AI has brought to SEO is the rise of zero-click searches. More users now get answers directly on search engine results pages (SERPs) without clicking through to a website. Google's featured snippets, knowledge panels, and AI-driven answers make optimizing for these elements crucial to maintaining visibility and traffic.

Additionally, Google's emphasis on **E-E-A-T (Experience, Expertise, Authority, and Trustworthiness)** underscores the importance of high-quality content. AI evaluates content credibility through various signals, favoring sources that demonstrate real-world expertise and trustworthiness. Websites that fail to align with E-E-A-T principles may struggle to rank, regardless of traditional SEO efforts.

Understanding and implementing AI-powered strategies for zero-click searches and E-E-A-T optimization is vital for staying ahead in the ever-changing SEO landscape.

What You Will Learn from This Book

This book is designed to equip you with cutting-edge knowledge and practical strategies for thriving in AI-driven SEO. You will learn:

- How AI is reshaping SEO and content marketing.
- The mechanics behind zero-click searches and how to optimize for them.
- The role of E-E-A-T in ranking and how to build authority.
- AI-driven keyword research and content optimization techniques.
- How machine learning impacts search algorithms and ranking factors.
- The future of AI in SEO and how to stay ahead of trends.

How You Will Benefit

By the end of this book, you will have a comprehensive understanding of AI-powered SEO and the tools needed to implement successful strategies. Whether you are a business owner, marketer, content creator, or SEO professional, mastering AI in SEO will enable you to:

- Enhance your website's visibility in AI-driven search results.
- Improve content credibility and authority.

- Drive organic traffic despite the rise of zero-click searches.
- Leverage AI tools to streamline SEO efforts.
- Future-proof your SEO strategies in an evolving digital world.

Get ready to embrace the AI revolution in SEO and take your digital presence to the next level!

Chapter 1: Understanding the AI-Driven SEO Landscape

The Rise of AI in SEO

Introduction to AI in SEO

Artificial Intelligence (AI) is revolutionizing Search Engine Optimization (SEO), changing how search engines rank content and how users interact with search results. From **machine learning algorithms** to **natural language processing (NLP)**, AI-powered tools like Google's RankBrain and BERT are reshaping digital marketing strategies.

Key AI Innovations in SEO:

- **AI-Powered Content Creation**: Tools like GPT-based models and AI-assisted writing improve content relevance and quality.
- **Predictive Search & Personalization**: Search engines leverage AI to tailor results based on user history and behavior.
- **Automated Technical SEO**: AI helps in optimizing site structure, identifying broken links, and improving Core Web Vitals.
- **Voice and Visual Search**: AI enhances the accuracy of voice queries and image-based searches.

By leveraging AI, businesses can enhance their **E-E-A-T (Experience, Expertise, Authority, and Trust)** to rank higher and build credibility in their niche.

How AI is Changing Search Behavior

AI-Driven Personalization and Search Intent

Search engines are now more adept at understanding **search intent**—whether informational, navigational, transactional, or commercial. AI analyzes vast amounts of user data, identifying patterns to deliver hyper-relevant search results.

Impacts of AI on Search Behavior:

- **Conversational Search**: With advancements in NLP, search queries are becoming more natural and question-based.
- **Hyper-Personalization**: Google and Bing use AI to tailor search results based on location, device, browsing history, and preferences.
- **Contextual Understanding**: AI improves query interpretation through semantic search, identifying the true intent behind keywords.

To stay competitive, content creators must optimize for **AI-friendly search queries**, using structured data, long-tail keywords, and natural language.

The Role of AI in Zero-Click Searches

What Are Zero-Click Searches?

A **zero-click search** occurs when users find answers directly in search engine results without clicking through to a website. This happens through:

- **Featured Snippets** (Position Zero results)
- **Knowledge Panels**
- **People Also Ask (PAA) Sections**
- **Local Packs & Instant Answers**

How AI Powers Zero-Click Search Results

Search engines extract high-quality, authoritative information to display in zero-click features. AI identifies the most relevant content using:

- **Entity Recognition & Semantic Search**: AI determines the best sources to answer user queries concisely.
- **Natural Language Generation (NLG)**: AI summarizes content into snippet-ready formats.

- **User Intent Matching**: AI prioritizes responses that align with search behavior.

Optimizing for Zero-Click Search Readiness

To maximize visibility in AI-driven search results:

1. **Optimize for Featured Snippets**: Use structured content with clear, concise answers.
2. **Implement Schema Markup**: Utilize structured data (e.g., FAQ, How-To, Breadcrumbs) to help search engines understand content better.
3. **Improve E-E-A-T Signals**: Ensure content reflects expertise, authority, and trustworthiness.
4. **Leverage Conversational and Question-Based Content**: Use **H2/H3 headings** in Q&A format to align with People Also Ask sections.
5. **Enhance Mobile & Voice Search Optimization**: AI-driven search heavily relies on **voice-friendly content** and **mobile-first indexing**.

Final Thoughts

The AI-driven SEO landscape is evolving rapidly, requiring marketers and content creators to adapt. By embracing AI tools, optimizing for zero-click searches, and strengthening E-E-A-T, businesses can remain competitive in an AI-first search ecosystem. The key is to align content strategies with AI-driven search intent, structured data, and **user-first content approaches** to secure a **top-ranking position in search results.**

Chapter 2: Zero-Click Searches – The New SEO Frontier

What Are Zero-Click Searches?

Zero-click searches occur when users find the information they need directly on the search engine results page (SERP) without clicking through to a website. These results are often displayed in featured snippets, knowledge panels, and answer boxes, minimizing the need for users to visit external sites.

The Impact on SEO

Zero-click searches are transforming SEO by shifting traffic away from traditional organic results and toward SERP features controlled by search engines. Websites must now optimize content to appear in these high-visibility areas to remain competitive and relevant.

How AI Optimizes for Zero-Click Searches

AI plays a crucial role in structuring content to rank in zero-click positions. Search engines use AI-driven algorithms to analyze content and extract direct answers. Businesses leveraging AI can improve their content's chances of being featured.

AI-Powered Optimization Techniques

1. **Featured Snippets:** AI can analyze search trends and suggest how to format content for featured snippets.
2. **Knowledge Graphs:** AI helps structure data in a way that is easily digestible for search engines.
3. **Answer Boxes:** AI-generated content can improve the accuracy and relevance of direct answers.
4. **Voice Search Optimization:** AI tools can refine responses to match conversational queries, which often trigger zero-click results.

Practical Strategies for Dominating Zero-Click Searches

To secure zero-click search positions, businesses should focus on the following strategies:

1. Structuring Content for Featured Snippets

- Use **clear, concise headings** (H2, H3, bullet points, and lists).
- Answer **common questions directly** at the beginning of paragraphs.
- Provide **step-by-step instructions** for procedural queries.

2. Implementing Schema Markup

- Use **structured data** to help search engines understand the context.
- Implement **FAQ, How-To, and Q&A schema** to enhance visibility.
- Leverage **structured product data** for eCommerce zero-click searches.

3. Crafting Concise and Direct Answers

- Keep answers **brief yet informative** (40-60 words for featured snippets).
- Use **data-backed insights** and industry authority to enhance credibility.
- Ensure **content clarity** to match user intent effectively.

4. Enhancing User Experience for AI-Driven Search

- Improve **mobile-friendliness** to match voice search results.
- Optimize **loading speed** to enhance search engine ranking.
- Focus on **natural language processing (NLP)** techniques to improve readability.

Case Studies: AI-Driven Success in Zero-Click Optimization

Case Study 1: E-Commerce Site Boosting Featured Snippets

An e-commerce brand used AI-generated structured content to optimize product descriptions. By integrating schema markup and direct-answer formatting, the brand increased its featured snippet presence by 40%, leading to a higher conversion rate despite lower click-through rates.

Case Study 2: Healthcare Blog Leveraging AI for Answer Boxes

A medical website implemented AI tools to format articles in a way that fit Google's answer box criteria. By refining content using AI-driven keyword analysis and concise summaries, the site saw a 30% increase in zero-click appearances, reinforcing its authority in the industry.

Case Study 3: Local Business Enhancing Knowledge Graph Visibility

A local business optimized its Google My Business profile and used AI-powered keyword research to align its descriptions with common zero-click queries. This resulted in an increased knowledge graph presence, driving more foot traffic and calls.

Conclusion

Zero-click searches are redefining SEO, shifting the focus from traditional rankings to strategic content structuring. Businesses must embrace AI-driven optimization techniques to stay visible in an evolving digital landscape. By leveraging structured data, concise answers, and AI-powered insights, content creators can adapt to this new SEO frontier and maintain a competitive edge.

Chapter 3: E-E-A-T – Building Trust in an AI-Driven World

What is E-E-A-T (Experience, Expertise, Authority, Trust)?

- **Understanding E-E-A-T**: E-E-A-T is a framework used by Google to evaluate the quality of content and how it should be ranked. It's particularly relevant for content in "Your Money or Your Life" (YMYL) categories, where misinformation can lead to serious consequences. It evaluates four main pillars:
  - **Experience**: The direct experience someone has with a subject (e.g., first-hand accounts, field work, or practical application). For example, a recipe blog that shares personal cooking experiences demonstrates experience.
  - **Expertise**: The depth of knowledge and credentials in a particular subject. This could be a professional's technical knowledge, research-based content, or credentials like certifications or degrees.
  - **Authority**: The perceived credibility of the content creator and their website. Authority is gained by being

mentioned by reputable sources, gaining backlinks, and having recognition in the community. For example, a medical blog backed by a renowned doctor is seen as more authoritative.

- o **Trust**: How reliable and dependable your content is, often tied to factors like accuracy, transparency, and reliability. Trust can be built through authentic reviews, clear contact information, and up-to-date content.

- **How Google Uses E-E-A-T**: Google evaluates these factors primarily through human raters and AI algorithms to rank websites. It looks for signals of high E-E-A-T in several ways:

  - o **Content Quality**: Is the content comprehensive, accurate, and well-written?

  - o **Author Information**: Does the author have credentials or recognizable expertise in the field?

  - o **Backlinks and Citations**: Are the sources cited authoritative and trustworthy?

  - o **User Signals**: Does the content have high engagement, and are users returning for more?

- Site Design and Security: Is the website secure (HTTPS), easy to navigate, and user-friendly?

AI's Role in E-E-A-T Optimization

- **AI Tools for Content Creation**: AI has become integral in improving content quality, creating valuable experiences for users, and optimizing content for SEO and E-E-A-T. Several AI-powered tools can support E-E-A-T optimization:
  - **Content Generation**: AI can help produce high-quality content based on a deep understanding of topics. Tools like GPT-based models can generate articles, blog posts, and reports, but they can also be refined to focus on high E-E-A-T by integrating facts, expert quotes, and sources.
  - **Semantic Analysis and Keyword Research**: AI can analyze user intent, find relevant keywords, and identify content gaps. By understanding how people search for specific topics and optimizing content accordingly, AI helps improve content relevance.
  - **Content Grading**: AI tools like Hemingway or Grammarly not only help with grammar but can analyze

content for readability, tone, and overall quality, helping to meet user expectations and trust.

- o **Topic Generation**: AI can identify trending topics, search volume, and subject matter that resonate with audiences, making sure the content you create is relevant and shows expertise in the field.
- o **AI-Powered Fact-Checking**: AI can verify sources and check facts, ensuring content is accurate, which is essential for building trust.

- **Automated Research and Expertise**: AI tools can scan a wide variety of sources quickly and suggest authoritative references and articles that can be linked to your content. Tools like **IBM Watson** and **Google's Natural Language API** can help identify credible academic sources, government websites, or recognized industry publications to cite.

- o **Citing Research and Data**: AI tools like **QuillBot** and **Grammarly** also help with rephrasing and summarizing complex research into digestible information that enhances your content's expertise without sacrificing quality.
- o **Content Benchmarking**: AI can analyze competitor websites,

identifying what type of content they're publishing, how it ranks, and how authoritative their sources are. This helps you match or exceed industry standards for authority.

Creating Content that Meets E-E-A-T

- **Step-by-Step Guide**:
  1. **Demonstrating Experience**:
     - Use personal case studies, interviews, and testimonials to showcase practical experience. AI can analyze large volumes of data to identify patterns in user behavior and can help write case studies that reflect real-world applications of the topic.
     - **AI Tip**: Use **ChatGPT** or similar AI tools to summarize real-life stories or interviews, adding them to your content as relatable examples that resonate with readers.
  2. **Showcasing Expertise**:
     - Incorporate authoritative references and well-researched information into your content. Use AI tools to analyze the top-ranking articles and gather data from credible sources.

- **AI Tip**: Tools like **SurferSEO** or **Frase** can help with content research, ensuring the content is both comprehensive and optimized for SEO by suggesting authoritative sources.

3. **Building Authority**:
   - Gain backlinks from reputable websites, such as industry blogs or news outlets. AI can help identify authoritative websites in your niche and suggest opportunities for collaboration, guest posts, or link-building strategies.
   - **AI Tip**: Use **Ahrefs** or **SEMrush** to monitor backlinks, and AI tools can suggest high-authority sites to reach out to.

4. **Establishing Trust**:
   - Add trust signals to your content such as privacy policies, security badges, and credible external sources. AI can also help track the reliability of your sources and ensure content is up-to-date.
   - **AI Tip**: AI-powered chatbots can collect user reviews or testimonials, directly

enhancing trust by showcasing positive experiences.

How AI Helps Establish Trust

- **Behavioral Analysis**: AI tools track user engagement to understand how they interact with your content. For example, an AI-powered website analytics tool can monitor metrics like bounce rates, session durations, and page interactions.
  - ○ **AI Tip**: Use **Hotjar** or **Crazy Egg** to monitor how users engage with your content and make adjustments to improve their experience.
  - ○ **Adjust Content Based on Behavior**: Based on these insights, AI can suggest adjustments to content such as changing headlines, refining CTA placement, or offering additional resources, which can increase trust.
- **Improving Trust Signals**:
  - ○ **Reviews & Testimonials**: AI tools like **Trustpilot** or **Yelp API** can aggregate customer reviews and analyze sentiment, helping you understand how customers feel about your content or products.
  - ○ **Security and Transparency**: AI can automate the display of important trust signals such as security badges,

company credentials, or author bios. Tools like **Cloudflare** can ensure security while **Google Structured Data** helps present trust signals like reviews and expert qualifications in search results.

- ○ **AI-Personalized Content**: AI can personalize your website's user experience by tailoring content recommendations or product suggestions based on past behaviors, increasing the relevance and trustworthiness of your content.

Practical Example for AI-Driven E-E-A-T Optimization

Scenario: A health and wellness blog looking to optimize for E-E-A-T.

1. **Experience**: AI analyzes user search queries and finds common health issues people are looking to solve (e.g., sleep improvement). AI generates blog posts with personal success stories or real user-generated content (testimonials).
2. **Expertise**: AI uses a health database like PubMed to fetch the latest research on sleep improvement. The blog includes expert

quotes and links to reputable studies, ensuring that the content is grounded in verified scientific knowledge.

3. **Authority**: AI recommends high-authority sites and influencers in the health field. The blog publishes guest posts by a licensed sleep therapist, gaining backlinks from trusted health-related sites.

4. **Trust**: AI analyzes user behavior, identifying that readers are most interested in sleep tips. It suggests adding trust-building content like security badges (e.g., privacy policy) and links to trusted health organizations.

Chapter 4: Combining AI with Zero-Click Optimization for Maximum Impact

Merging AI with Zero-Click: How to Align AI-Powered Content Creation with Zero-Click Search Strategies

- **Understanding Zero-Click Searches**:
  - A **Zero-Click Search** occurs when users get the answer they're looking for directly from a search engine's results page (SERP), without needing to click through to a website. These can include Featured Snippets, Knowledge Panels, Local Packs, and more.
  - Why Zero-Click is Crucial for SEO: Zero-click results provide immediate, relevant answers, driving visibility and increasing authority. It's also a sign of expertise, as Google is presenting your content directly to users.
- **Aligning AI Content with Zero-Click Strategies**:
  - **AI-Driven Content Creation**: AI can be harnessed to create content specifically designed to answer the types of questions users are asking, which is essential for ranking in Zero-Click results.

- **AI-Powered Research**: Tools like **GPT-3**, **BERT** (for understanding user intent), and **AnswerThePublic** can help identify the most frequently asked questions in your niche, guiding content creation.
- **Conversational Content**: AI helps generate content that's clear, concise, and to the point—perfect for Featured Snippets and other Zero-Click formats.

○ **Format Alignment**: The format of Zero-Click content can vary—whether it's a brief definition, list, or how-to guide. AI tools can automatically format content into these structures, making it more likely to be pulled into Zero-Click positions.

- **Example**: AI might structure content into concise answers (for "What is..." queries), bulleted lists (for comparison queries), or step-by-step instructions (for "How to" queries).

AI Tools for Enhanced Zero-Click Optimization

- **GPT-3 and Natural Language Processing (NLP)**:
    - **GPT-3** (and other AI language models) can be used to generate high-quality, concise content optimized for Zero-Click formats. By training the AI on vast amounts of data, it can craft content tailored to answer user queries with precision.
        - **How GPT-3 Helps**: You can feed GPT-3 specific prompts (e.g., "Create a concise list of the benefits of meditation"), and it will generate content in the right format for a Zero-Click search result.
    - **NLP for Query Understanding**: NLP allows AI to understand the exact context of user queries and deliver content that directly answers those needs. For example, NLP algorithms can detect user intent more accurately, crafting content that fits within the context of "What," "How," and "Why" questions commonly featured in Zero-Click results.
        - **Example**: If users search "best dog food for allergies," NLP tools can ensure that the AI-

generated content is focused on allergy-related dog food options in a structured list format.

- **AI Content Optimization Tools**:
  - **Frase**, **SurferSEO**, and **RankMath**: These tools use AI to analyze the top-ranking content for Zero-Click queries. They can identify gaps and suggest modifications that make your content more likely to appear in featured snippets or other Zero-Click results.
    - **Example**: Frase's AI-powered content planner can suggest the best structure and keywords to optimize your content for snippet inclusion.
  - **AI for Semantic Search**: AI can optimize content by understanding semantic relationships between terms, ensuring that it answers all the nuances of a query. This is especially helpful for appearing in **People Also Ask** boxes and **Knowledge Graph** results.
    - **Example**: NLP tools can create content that not only answers the main query but also anticipates follow-up questions

and includes those answers in an expandable FAQ section.

Structured Data and Schema Markup: Using AI to Automatically Generate Structured Data and Schema for Better Visibility in Google's Rich Snippets

- **What is Structured Data and Schema Markup?**:
  - Structured data and schema markup are tags added to a webpage's HTML code that help search engines understand the context of the content. These tags make it easier for search engines to present content in rich snippets (e.g., star ratings, product information, event dates).
  - Examples of **Schema Markup**: Articles, local business information, recipes, reviews, FAQs, how-tos, etc.
- **Leveraging AI to Automate Structured Data Generation**:
  - **AI-Driven Schema Generation**: AI tools can automatically generate schema markup based on the content's structure and context. For example, once AI analyzes an article about a specific product, it can tag relevant information (price, rating, availability) using schema.

- **Automating Rich Snippets**: By combining AI-powered content creation with schema generation, you increase the chances of your content being pulled into rich snippets. For example, **Yoast SEO** and **RankMath** offer features where AI detects content that can be marked up with structured data.
- **AI and JSON-LD**: AI tools can help generate structured data using **JSON-LD** (JavaScript Object Notation for Linked Data), the format that Google prefers for schema markup.
  - **Example**: If you have a recipe blog, AI can automatically generate recipe schema (ingredients, instructions, preparation time) so Google can display your recipe in a rich snippet with ratings, cooking time, etc.
- **Enhancing Knowledge Graph Visibility**: With schema markup and AI-powered analysis, your content can also appear in Google's Knowledge Graph, boosting your authority.

Real-Life Examples: Successful Zero-Click Optimizations that Leveraged AI-Driven Content Creation

- **Example 1: How an E-commerce Site Optimized Product Pages for Zero-Click**:
  - o A major e-commerce website used AI-powered tools to automatically generate FAQs based on user queries (e.g., "How do I return a product?"). They structured these FAQs using schema markup. This approach led to their content appearing in the **People Also Ask** section of Google, driving significant traffic without requiring users to click.
  - o **AI's Role**: The AI analyzed common queries, generated optimized content, and marked up the FAQs with schema, boosting visibility in Zero-Click results.
- **Example 2: Recipe Blog Using AI for Featured Snippets**:
  - o A recipe blog used GPT-3 to generate structured recipe content, breaking down the ingredients, steps, and tips in a highly structured manner. By using schema for recipes (with cooking time, serving size, etc.), they consistently ranked in **Rich Snippets** for highly competitive recipe queries.

- o **AI's Role**: GPT-3 optimized the recipe structure to match Zero-Click requirements, and schema markup ensured the content was recognized by Google as a rich snippet.
- **Example 3: Healthcare Site Achieving Knowledge Panel Inclusion**:
  - o A healthcare blog used AI to generate authoritative, concise answers to medical questions. They then applied **FAQ schema markup**, making the content eligible for the Knowledge Panel.
  - o **AI's Role**: The AI analyzed search intent, generated medically accurate, concise answers, and automatically tagged them with structured data.

Practical Tips for Combining AI with Zero-Click Optimization

1. **Focus on User Intent**: Use AI tools to understand the intent behind the query. Ensure your content addresses the specific need in the most direct way possible.
2. **Structured Content**: Organize your content into clear, digestible sections like lists, definitions, or steps—formats that perform well in Zero-Click results.

3. **Optimize for Rich Snippets**: Implement structured data (schema markup) for all relevant content (e.g., recipes, product pages, articles).
4. **Leverage AI for Continuous Updates**: AI can keep track of how content is performing in Zero-Click positions and suggest optimizations, such as reformatting or adding new information.

Chapter 5: AI-Driven Analytics – Measuring Your SEO Success

AI-Powered Analytics: How to Use AI to Track and Analyze SEO Performance, User Behavior, and Ranking Trends

- **The Role of AI in SEO Analytics**:
  - AI-powered analytics tools are revolutionizing how we track SEO performance, making it easier to interpret vast amounts of data and generate actionable insights. Traditional SEO analytics tools focus mainly on tracking keyword rankings, traffic, and backlinks, but AI tools bring a new dimension by analyzing user intent, predicting trends, and automating insights.
- **Key Metrics for Measuring SEO Success**:
  - **Organic Traffic**: AI tools can segment organic traffic based on various factors like demographics, geography, and behavior. By tracking which types of content generate the most engagement, AI helps prioritize future content strategies.
  - **Rankings and Keyword Performance**: AI tracks keyword movements in real-time, providing insights into what's working and

what's not, and predicting the next high-performing keywords.

- ○ **Bounce Rate and Dwell Time**: AI can analyze user behavior on the site—such as how long users stay on a page (dwell time) or how often they leave quickly (bounce rate)—and offer suggestions to improve user engagement.
- ○ **Click-Through Rate (CTR)**: AI tools like **SurferSEO** or **Frase** track how often your content appears in search results and how likely it is to be clicked, offering suggestions for improving headlines, meta descriptions, and overall visibility.

- **Behavioral Analysis**:
  - ○ AI-powered platforms can segment user behavior more accurately, tracking interactions with specific content, pages, or products. This helps you understand which parts of your website or content are resonating with visitors and which areas need improvement.
  - ○ Tools like **Hotjar** or **Crazy Egg** can provide heatmaps, scroll maps, and user recordings, revealing which sections of your content are engaging or being ignored.

Optimizing Your Strategy in Real-Time: How AI Analytics Can Provide Insights into Search Intent, Keyword Optimization, and Competitive Analysis

- **Search Intent Analysis**:
    - AI tools can understand and categorize **search intent**, such as informational, transactional, navigational, or commercial intent. This allows you to tailor your content to match what users are actually looking for, improving rankings and user experience.
    - For example, if a search intent is primarily informational (e.g., "How does AI work?"), AI tools can recommend creating a detailed guide or FAQ on the topic to address the user's needs directly.
    - **AI Tools for Intent Analysis**: Platforms like **Frase** and **ClearScope** use AI to identify content gaps by analyzing search intent behind top-ranking pages, helping you optimize your content strategy based on what users are really searching for.
- **Keyword Optimization with AI**:
    - AI can provide deeper insights into keyword performance, not just based on search volume but also on user

behavior, seasonal trends, and latent semantic indexing (LSI) keywords.

- ○ **AI-Powered Keyword Analysis**: Tools like **SEMrush**, **Ahrefs**, or **Moz** integrate AI to suggest keywords that are aligned with your SEO goals, track keyword trends, and identify emerging search patterns. They can also help predict long-tail keyword opportunities, offering insights into niche areas of potential traffic.
- ○ **Automating Keyword Optimization**: AI can help automate the optimization process by recommending the best keywords for specific pieces of content and adjusting keywords in real-time based on current performance.
- **Competitive Analysis with AI**:
  - ○ AI tools can analyze competitor websites, providing real-time data on their SEO strategies, backlink profiles, and content performance. This enables you to identify competitor strengths and weaknesses and adjust your strategy accordingly.
  - ○ **AI for Competitor Benchmarking**: Platforms like **SpyFu**, **SEMrush**, or **Ahrefs** utilize AI to track your competitors' SEO rankings, uncovering opportunities to target

low-hanging fruit or areas where your competitors are outperforming you.

- o **Competitive Gap Analysis**: AI can detect gaps in content or keywords that your competitors are ranking for, but you aren't. By analyzing these gaps, you can focus on creating content that meets both your target audience's needs and those of the competitive landscape.

Predictive Analytics: Using AI to Predict SEO Trends, Helping You Stay Ahead of Algorithm Updates and Shifts in Search Behavior

- **The Power of Predictive Analytics**:
  - o Predictive analytics powered by AI allows you to forecast SEO trends before they occur, giving you a competitive edge. AI uses historical data, user behavior patterns, and algorithm updates to predict future ranking trends, helping you adapt your SEO strategies proactively rather than reactively.
- **AI in SEO Trend Prediction**:
  - o **Trend Identification**: AI can analyze patterns in search behavior (e.g., rising topics, seasonal searches, or new Google algorithm changes) and help you predict which topics will

dominate search results in the coming months.

- o **Algorithm Update Predictions**: AI models can monitor Google's algorithm updates and suggest changes to your SEO strategy. For example, if a major algorithm update is likely to prioritize **E-E-A-T** (Experience, Expertise, Authority, Trust), AI might recommend adjusting your content for better authority signals and trustworthiness.
- **Using Predictive Analytics for Content Strategy**:
  - o AI can also forecast which types of content will perform well based on current search trends. For instance, if AI identifies that "sustainable fashion" is becoming a trending topic, it can predict the kind of content (e.g., eco-friendly clothing guides) that will gain traction in SERPs.
  - o **Real-Time Adjustments**: AI can help track shifts in search volume, allowing you to quickly pivot your content or SEO strategy to capitalize on new opportunities or address search behavior changes.

Tools and Resources: Recommended AI-Powered SEO and Analytics Tools for Measuring Success and Refining Strategy

- **Google Analytics (with AI Features)**:
    - Google Analytics uses AI and machine learning models to offer more insightful reports on user behavior, traffic sources, and performance metrics. With AI-powered features like **Insights** and **Predictive Analytics**, Google Analytics can automatically suggest optimization opportunities and highlight emerging trends.
- **AI-Driven SEO Tools**:
    - **SurferSEO**: SurferSEO uses AI to analyze SERPs, suggest content optimizations, and provide keyword analysis based on real-time data.
    - **Frase**: An AI-powered content and SEO tool that helps optimize keyword strategies, analyze SERPs, and identify content gaps.
    - **ClearScope**: An AI content optimization tool that helps you identify the most relevant keywords, optimizing content for higher rankings by analyzing top-ranking pages.

- **AI Tools for Keyword Research**:
  - ○ **SEMrush**: SEMrush's AI-powered Keyword Magic Tool helps you find the best keywords based on search trends and competitor analysis, automatically suggesting keyword modifications.
  - ○ **Moz Pro**: Moz's Keyword Explorer, powered by AI, helps you find the most effective keywords and tracks their performance over time, making it easy to adjust your SEO strategy.
  - ○ **Ahrefs**: Ahrefs' AI-powered keyword research tool gives deep insights into search trends, keyword difficulty, and ranking potential.
- **AI for Competitor Analysis**:
  - ○ **SpyFu**: SpyFu uses AI to track competitors' SEO strategies and keyword performance, helping you adjust your strategy accordingly.
  - ○ **Ahrefs**: Provides AI-backed competitive analysis by showing how your competitors' content ranks, their backlink profiles, and their SEO tactics.
- **AI-Powered Predictive Analytics Tools**:
  - ○ **BrightEdge**: BrightEdge uses AI to predict trends in search and help you

adjust your strategy based on current data and algorithm changes.

- ○ **MarketMuse**: MarketMuse uses predictive analytics to suggest topics, content gaps, and keyword opportunities to stay ahead of competitors and forecast SEO trends.

Practical Tips for Using AI in SEO Analytics

1. **Integrate AI into Your Analytics Workflow**: Use AI tools for automated keyword tracking, traffic analysis, and competitor research to streamline your SEO efforts.
2. **Leverage Predictive Analytics**: Stay ahead of trends by incorporating predictive AI insights into your content strategy, anticipating shifts in search behavior.
3. **Real-Time Data Analysis**: Use AI analytics tools to monitor your SEO performance in real-time, making adjustments to your strategy instantly as trends evolve.

Chapter 6: The Future of SEO – Adapting to AI and Search Algorithm Changes

How AI Will Continue to Shape SEO: Exploring Emerging Trends in AI, Voice Search, Machine Learning, and How They'll Affect SEO Strategies

- **AI and SEO – A Symbiotic Relationship**:
    - AI has already had a profound impact on SEO, and its role will only continue to grow. As AI tools become more sophisticated, they'll offer better ways to predict search trends, optimize content for voice search, and enhance user engagement.
    - AI's influence on SEO is expanding through **machine learning** (ML), which allows search engines like Google to understand context, user intent, and the relationships between different pieces of content, rather than just relying on keyword matching.
- **Voice Search Optimization**:
    - With the rise of **virtual assistants** (Siri, Alexa, Google Assistant) and **voice-enabled devices**, optimizing for voice search is becoming critical. Voice search queries tend to be more conversational, longer, and context-

driven, which will affect the way you create content.

- AI's Role: Voice search relies heavily on AI to process natural language, and this is a crucial area for SEO in the future. Marketers will need to optimize for more natural, conversational phrases and structure content in ways that align with how users interact with voice assistants.
    - Example: Instead of optimizing for keywords like "best pizza near me," voice search optimization might focus on "Where can I find the best pizza near me that's open late?"

- **Machine Learning and Predictive Search**:
    - **Machine learning** will allow search engines to predict user behavior and deliver results that anticipate the user's intent even before they finish typing. AI algorithms can analyze patterns in past searches and user actions to deliver more personalized search results.
    - **Example**: Machine learning-powered systems like Google's RankBrain and BERT are already improving how Google interprets context and user intent in search queries. Marketers will need to adapt by optimizing

content to address not just keywords but the deeper meanings behind searches.

- **AI and Content Personalization**:
    - ○ **Content personalization** will take center stage as AI continues to understand individual user preferences. Search engines will prioritize delivering hyper-relevant, personalized results based on past behavior, location, and search history.
    - ○ **SEO Strategy Shift**: This means that SEO strategies will have to shift from broad keyword optimization to delivering personalized content that adapts to the preferences of individual users.
        - ▪ **AI's Role**: Using AI to analyze and segment audiences will help create personalized experiences and optimize for long-tail keywords and niche searches.

The Role of Zero-Click and E-E-A-T in the Future of SEO: Predictions for the Continued

Relevance of Zero-Click and E-E-A-T, and How to Future-Proof Your Content

- **Zero-Click Searches: Growing Relevance**:
  - ○ **Zero-click searches** will likely continue to dominate search results, particularly as **Google's Featured Snippets**, **Knowledge Panels**, and **People Also Ask** boxes become more sophisticated.
  - ○ **AI's Impact**: AI will refine how Google extracts and displays information directly on the search results page. As AI helps Google understand content more deeply, Zero-Click results will become even more precise and accurate, pushing businesses to focus on optimizing their content for these formats.
  - ○ **Future-Proofing Content for Zero-Click**:
    - ▪ Create content that answers common questions succinctly.
    - ▪ Focus on providing **direct answers**, **concise summaries**, and **structured content** (bullet points, how-tos) to increase the chances of being selected as a Zero-Click result.
    - ▪ **AI Tools** like **Frase** and **AnswerThePublic** can help

identify which queries are most likely to trigger Zero-Click results and guide content creation accordingly.

- **E-E-A-T – The Key to Staying Ahead in SEO**:
  - **Experience, Expertise, Authority, and Trust** (E-E-A-T) will continue to be central to SEO as Google refines its algorithms to prioritize high-quality content.
  - **AI's Role**: AI tools can help assess content quality by identifying signals of trust and authority. For example, AI can evaluate backlinks, user-generated content (e.g., reviews), and the credibility of your content by cross-referencing with authoritative sources.
    - **Building E-E-A-T with AI**: Using AI-powered tools, businesses can automatically optimize their content to enhance trust signals (like displaying testimonials, featuring author bios with credentials, and using high-authority references).
- **How to Prepare for the Future of E-E-A-T**:

- Ensure your content is **well-researched**, **authored by experts**, and **transparent** (e.g., clear references to credible sources, an About page with author credentials).
- AI can be used to audit content for gaps in E-E-A-T, ensuring all aspects of content quality are up to par, from providing accurate information to including proper citations.

Adapting to Algorithm Changes: How AI Will Help You Quickly Adjust Your SEO Strategies in Response to Future Google Algorithm Updates

- **The Challenge of Algorithm Updates**:
  - Google's algorithms evolve frequently, and SEO professionals need to be agile in responding to updates. Major algorithm updates, such as **Core Web Vitals** and **Mobile-First Indexing**, have already changed the SEO landscape, and more updates are expected.
- **AI and Algorithm Change Prediction**:
  - AI can help you stay ahead of the curve by predicting potential algorithm shifts. By analyzing historical data and tracking patterns in Google's updates, AI-powered tools

can forecast which changes are likely to affect SEO strategies.

- o **AI's Role in Response**:
  - ▪ **Real-Time Adjustments**: AI tools can automatically adjust content, keywords, and technical SEO elements based on the latest algorithm shifts. For instance, AI can suggest changes in page speed, content length, or keyword optimization in response to Google's Core Web Vitals update.
  - ▪ **Automating Content Reoptimization**: AI-driven platforms can re-optimize your existing content automatically, ensuring your website stays aligned with Google's evolving ranking factors.
- • **Anticipating Future Algorithm Changes**:
  - o **AI Analysis**: By continuously analyzing data and trends, AI can identify changes in how Google is prioritizing content. These insights allow you to adapt quickly, ensuring your site remains competitive even in the face of future updates.

Preparing for the Long-Term: Preparing Your Digital Strategy to Thrive in an AI-Driven SEO Future

- **Embracing an AI-Driven SEO Approach**:
    - As AI becomes integral to SEO, it's essential to build a strategy that leverages AI tools for content creation, keyword research, optimization, and performance tracking. Businesses that fail to embrace AI risk being left behind.
    - **How AI Will Continue to Shape Long-Term SEO**:
        - Automating repetitive SEO tasks (content generation, keyword analysis, performance tracking).
        - Continuously optimizing content to meet emerging trends and user intent.
        - Using predictive analytics to forecast changes in search behavior and adjust strategies accordingly.
- **Focus on User Experience (UX)**:
    - **User experience** will become even more important as AI helps Google assess how visitors interact with your site. Websites that provide fast loading times, easy navigation, and

relevant, high-quality content will continue to thrive in the future SEO landscape.

- o AI can help improve **site usability** by analyzing user behavior and recommending design adjustments.

- **AI-Powered Content Strategy for the Future**:
  - o Continuously evolve your content strategy to address shifting trends. **Content personalization**, **hyper-relevant content**, and **dynamic content strategies** will become essential.
  - o AI can help create content that adapts in real-time to users' preferences, enhancing the user experience and increasing engagement.

- **Building a Future-Proof SEO Strategy**:
  - o **Diversify Your Content Formats**: With AI helping optimize for both traditional and new formats (like voice search and video), create a variety of content types to stay competitive.
  - o **Focus on E-E-A-T**: Consistently update content to maintain authority, trustworthiness, and relevance. Use AI to help you identify

content gaps and enhance trust signals.

Practical Tips for Future-Proofing Your SEO Strategy

1. **Leverage AI for Real-Time Adaptation**: Use AI tools to monitor algorithm changes, track ranking shifts, and adjust your strategy on the fly.
2. **Prepare for the Rise of Voice Search**: Optimize content for voice search by focusing on natural, conversational phrases.
3. **Embrace AI-Powered Content Personalization**: Use AI to deliver hyper-targeted, personalized content that resonates with your audience.
4. **Focus on E-E-A-T**: Prioritize high-quality, authoritative, and trustworthy content that meets Google's standards.

Chapter 7: Actionable AI SEO Strategy for Long-Term Success

Building Your AI SEO Plan: How to Create a Cohesive, Long-Term Strategy Using AI for Zero-Click and E-E-A-T Optimization

- **Understanding the Big Picture**:
  - A successful long-term AI SEO strategy integrates **Zero-Click Search optimization** and **E-E-A-T (Experience, Expertise, Authority, Trust)**. These components are essential for maintaining visibility, meeting user intent, and building credibility in a competitive SEO landscape.
- **How AI Fits Into Your Strategy**:
  - **Zero-Click Search Optimization**: With AI's ability to analyze SERPs, you can create content tailored to fit Google's featured snippets, knowledge panels, and other Zero-Click formats. This helps you capture visibility at the top of search results and drive traffic even when users don't click through to your site.
    - **AI's Role**: AI tools can analyze search intent, user queries, and SERP features to recommend content structure,

formats (bullet points, tables, and concise answers), and keywords likely to trigger Zero-Click results.

- **Actionable Tip**: Use AI tools like **Frase** and **SurferSEO** to identify high-impact Zero-Click search queries in your niche and optimize your content accordingly.

o **E-E-A-T Optimization**: AI can automate the process of building authoritative and trustworthy content. By identifying credible sources, enhancing content quality, and ensuring transparency, AI tools help improve your website's E-E-A-T.

- **AI's Role**: Tools like **MarketMuse** and **ClearScope** analyze top-ranking pages to ensure your content aligns with Google's quality standards and builds authority.

- **Actionable Tip**: Use AI to audit existing content for gaps in E-E-A-T. Add expert author bios, reference authoritative sources, and make sure your content aligns with current trends to stay relevant.

- **Creating a Long-Term AI SEO Strategy**:

- **Content Plan Development**: Build a content plan that focuses on answering key questions, addressing long-tail keywords, and providing detailed, authoritative content that showcases your experience and expertise.
- **AI Tools for Ongoing Optimization**:
  - **Frase**: Automates content creation based on search intent and helps ensure that content matches both E-E-A-T and Zero-Click formats.
  - **SurferSEO**: Uses AI to optimize on-page content and structure for Zero-Click optimization, making it easier to get featured snippets.
- **Link Building and Backlink Strategy**:
  - AI-powered tools can automate the process of identifying link-building opportunities, ensuring your site receives backlinks from reputable, authoritative sources, further boosting your E-E-A-T score.
  - **AI for Backlinks**: **Ahrefs** and **SEMrush** can help identify high-quality backlink opportunities, monitor

backlinks, and analyze competitor link profiles.

Key Steps to Take Today: Actionable Recommendations for Businesses, Marketers, and Content Creators to Implement AI-Powered SEO Strategies Immediately

- **1. Optimize for Zero-Click Searches**:
  - Research the most common Zero-Click queries in your niche using **Frase** or **AnswerThePublic**.
  - Update existing content to directly answer questions in the **People Also Ask** sections, using concise, structured formats.
    - **Actionable Tip**: Focus on creating "What," "How," and "Why" sections with easily scannable bullet points and tables.
- **2. Improve E-E-A-T Signals**:
  - Add **authoritative sources** to all content, including expert quotes, citations, and up-to-date references.
  - Showcase **author expertise** by featuring author bios with credentials, links to social profiles, and links to other articles they've written.

- ▪ **Actionable Tip**: Audit your existing content for missing E-E-A-T signals, such as author credibility and trustworthiness signals (e.g., privacy policies, contact information, testimonials).
- ▪ **Use AI to assess your content**: Tools like **MarketMuse** and **Frase** will analyze the E-E-A-T quality of your content and suggest areas for improvement.
- **3. Leverage AI for Content Creation**:
  - ○ Use **AI-driven tools** like **Copy.ai**, **Jasper**, or **Writesonic** for efficient content generation, ensuring it aligns with SEO best practices and provides high-quality, engaging content that appeals to both users and search engines.
  - ○ AI can help optimize headlines, meta descriptions, and alt text to maximize your content's discoverability and appeal.
- **4. Enhance On-Page SEO with AI**:
  - ○ Use **SurferSEO** or **Clearscope** to optimize content for keyword density, structure, and context relevance. These tools offer AI-based suggestions to improve on-page SEO,

including keyword integration, readability, and internal linking.
  - ○ **Actionable Tip**: Focus on content that adds real value, answering complex user queries in depth. AI-powered tools can ensure your content is optimized to address all aspects of a search query.
- **5. Implement AI-Powered Analytics for Ongoing Optimization**:
  - ○ Use **Google Analytics** (with AI features) and tools like **BrightEdge** to track keyword performance, user behavior, and content engagement.
  - ○ Regularly analyze your AI insights to adjust content strategy, refine keyword targeting, and ensure alignment with both user intent and algorithmic changes.
    - ▪ **Actionable Tip**: Set up real-time dashboards to track performance, making it easier to make adjustments quickly based on AI insights.

Tools and Resources: A Roundup of Essential AI-Driven Tools for SEO, Content Creation, and Performance Tracking

- **AI-Powered SEO Tools**:
  - **SurferSEO**: Uses AI to analyze SERPs and suggests on-page optimizations to improve rankings. Ideal for targeting Zero-Click opportunities.
  - **Frase**: Leverages AI to optimize content for search intent, automate content creation, and improve SEO strategy.
  - **Ahrefs**: AI-powered backlink analysis and competitor research tool that helps identify link-building opportunities.
  - **SEMrush**: Offers AI-based keyword research, site audits, and competitive analysis.
  - **Moz Pro**: Provides AI-driven keyword insights, link building, and SEO audits.
- **AI Content Creation Tools**:
  - **Jasper**: AI tool for writing high-quality content tailored for SEO and user engagement.
  - **Writesonic**: Leverages AI for generating blog posts, landing pages, and more to improve content creation efficiency.

- o **Copy.ai**: Uses AI to create optimized marketing copy, headlines, and long-form content that aligns with SEO best practices.
- **AI Analytics and Tracking Tools**:
  - o **Google Analytics with AI Insights**: Google's AI-powered tool tracks user behavior, traffic sources, and engagement metrics, helping you make data-driven decisions.
  - o **MarketMuse**: AI-based content research and optimization tool that ensures your content is authoritative and aligns with SEO best practices.
  - o **ClearScope**: Uses AI to analyze SERPs and provide keyword optimization suggestions based on the top-ranking pages.

Creating a Sustainable SEO System: How to Continuously Optimize and Adjust Your Strategy for Consistent, Long-Term Growth

- **The Importance of Continuous Optimization**:
  - o SEO is an ongoing process. To maintain long-term success, continuously monitor and refine your strategy using AI insights, adapting

your approach to search engine algorithm updates and shifts in user behavior.

- **AI for Long-Term Optimization**:
  - **Monitor Performance**: Use AI-powered tools to track the performance of content, keywords, and user engagement regularly.
  - **Content Audits**: Set a schedule for regular content audits using AI to identify outdated or underperforming pages. Refine and re-optimize your content based on the latest trends and insights.
  - **AI for Trendspotting**: Predict trends in user behavior, keywords, and content performance using **AI-powered analytics** to stay ahead of the competition and shift your strategy when needed.
- **Maintain High E-E-A-T Standards**:
  - As AI continues to help improve SEO strategies, consistently focus on **E-E-A-T** by enhancing content with new expert insights, reliable citations, and authoritative sources.

Practical Tips for Building a Sustainable AI SEO Strategy

1. **Automate Repetitive SEO Tasks**: Use AI tools to automate keyword tracking, content optimization, and reporting, freeing up time for more strategic tasks.
2. **Stay Updated with Algorithm Changes**: Use AI to monitor and adjust your SEO strategy for any shifts in search behavior or algorithm updates.
3. **Optimize for Both Human Users and Search Engines**: Ensure that your content is high-quality, authoritative, and readable for human users, while also optimized for search engines.
4. **Build Long-Term Authority**: Focus on creating evergreen content that will continue to rank and provide value over time.

Conclusion: Becoming an AI-Powered SEO Expert

Recap of Key Concepts: Zero-Click Searches, E-E-A-T, and AI-Driven SEO

Throughout this guide, we've explored how **AI** is transforming SEO, especially in areas like **Zero-Click Searches**, **E-E-A-T**, and **AI-Driven Optimization**:

1. **Zero-Click Searches**: As Google continues to refine its SERP features, **Zero-Click** results—such as featured snippets, knowledge panels, and people also ask boxes—are becoming increasingly important. With AI tools, you can optimize your content to capture these positions, ensuring your website's visibility even when users don't click through to your site.

2. **E-E-A-T (Experience, Expertise, Authority, Trust)**: Google's focus on **E-E-A-T** highlights the importance of producing high-quality, authoritative, and trustworthy content. AI allows you to scale and automate the process of ensuring your content meets these criteria by analyzing competitor pages, tracking industry trends, and suggesting improvements for your content.

3. **AI-Driven SEO**: With the rise of AI, traditional SEO practices are being revolutionized. AI-powered tools streamline everything from content creation and keyword research to real-time optimization and analytics. As AI learns and adapts, it becomes a powerful ally for SEO professionals, automating tasks, identifying opportunities, and predicting trends.

Final Thoughts on the Future of SEO and AI's Ongoing Role in Shaping Digital Strategies

The future of SEO is undoubtedly intertwined with **AI**. As search engines become smarter, they prioritize **user intent**, **relevant content**, and **trustworthy sources**. AI plays a critical role in this evolution, offering insights and automation that will continue to shape SEO strategies for years to come.

- **Voice Search & Machine Learning**: As voice search and machine learning technologies advance, AI will help marketers refine their strategies to optimize for conversational keywords, long-tail searches, and context-based queries.
- **Content Personalization**: AI is also pushing the envelope on content

personalization. By analyzing user behavior, AI can help create highly targeted content that resonates with different segments of your audience, ensuring that your SEO strategy stays relevant in an ever-changing digital landscape.

- **Real-Time Adjustments**: As search algorithms evolve, AI will enable marketers to quickly adapt by identifying changes in ranking factors, search intent, and user behavior. This ensures that SEO strategies are always ahead of the curve, fostering continuous growth and optimization.

In short, **AI** is not just a tool for today; it is shaping the **SEO landscape** of tomorrow. Those who embrace AI-powered SEO will be better equipped to respond to algorithm changes, adapt to shifting user behaviors, and create content that remains relevant and authoritative.

How Mastering AI-Powered SEO Will Position You as a Leader in the Evolving SEO Space

Mastering **AI-powered SEO** is the key to staying ahead in the increasingly competitive digital space. By combining **Zero-Click Optimization**, **E-E-A-T principles**, and cutting-edge AI tools, you will gain a strategic advantage that sets you apart from competitors. Here's why mastering AI-driven SEO is essential:

1. **Efficiency**: AI streamlines SEO tasks, automating keyword research, content optimization, and performance tracking, saving time and resources. As a result, you can focus more on high-level strategy and content creation.

2. **Scalability**: AI allows for faster content creation, optimization, and tracking, enabling you to scale your SEO efforts across multiple projects, websites, or client portfolios without sacrificing quality.

3. **Adaptability**: As AI continues to evolve, so will the SEO landscape. By mastering AI-driven SEO now, you'll be prepared to adapt quickly to new trends, search engine updates, and shifts in user behavior.

4. **Thought Leadership**: Becoming proficient in AI SEO will position you as an expert in the field. You'll be able to not only optimize your own content but also provide valuable insights to clients, peers, and followers on the future of SEO.

Final Call to Action

To truly become an **AI-powered SEO expert**, it's time to take action. Embrace AI tools, experiment with strategies, and continuously refine your approach to SEO. Whether you're a business owner, content creator, or SEO professional, mastering these tools and concepts will allow you to thrive in the digital age and ensure long-term success in an AI-driven world.

As we look ahead, one thing is clear: AI isn't the future of SEO—it's the present. Embrace it, and position yourself at the forefront of this transformation.

Appendix: Resources for AI and SEO Tools

Below is a curated list of **AI-powered SEO tools**, **analytics platforms**, and **content creation tools** that will help you implement the strategies covered in this book. These tools are designed to streamline your SEO efforts, optimize your content, and provide actionable insights to improve performance.

---

1. AI-Powered SEO Tools

These tools leverage artificial intelligence to assist with keyword research, on-page SEO, backlink analysis, and SERP tracking.

- **Frase**
  Use for: Content research, keyword analysis, Zero-Click optimization, and content creation based on search intent. *Why it's useful*: Frase uses AI to analyze SERPs, recommend content structures, and automate content generation tailored to user queries and Google's ranking factors. Website
- **SurferSEO**
  Use for: On-page SEO optimization, keyword research, and content audit. *Why it's useful*: SurferSEO's AI-driven platform analyzes your content against top-

ranking pages and provides recommendations for keyword density, structure, and other SEO factors to improve rankings.
Website

- **MarketMuse**

Use for: Content strategy, optimization, and keyword research.
Why it's useful: MarketMuse uses AI to help you create content that meets both **E-E-A-T** and SEO standards, analyzing the top-ranking pages to suggest keyword clusters and content improvements.
Website

- **Clearscope**

Use for: Keyword research, content optimization, and improving content quality.
Why it's useful: Clearscope's AI assists with keyword analysis and content optimization to ensure your content is top-quality, readable, and ranks well in SERPs.
Website

- **Ahrefs**

Use for: Backlink analysis, competitor research, and keyword tracking.
Why it's useful: While Ahrefs isn't fully AI-driven, it uses advanced algorithms to deliver insights into backlink profiles, keyword rankings, and site audits.
Website

- **SEMrush**

  Use for: Keyword research, SEO audits, and competitive analysis.

  Why it's useful: SEMrush combines AI and machine learning to offer a suite of tools that help you monitor SEO performance, find keyword opportunities, and stay competitive.

  Website

- **Moz** **Pro**

  Use for: Keyword tracking, SEO audits, and link building.

  Why it's useful: Moz Pro uses AI to track keyword rankings and offer insights into on-page SEO and backlink profiles. Website

---

2. AI-Powered Content Creation Tools

These tools help automate content writing and improve the quality of your blog posts, landing pages, and other digital content.

- **Jasper** (formerly Jarvis)

  Use for: Content generation, blog posts, and social media copywriting.

  Why it's useful: Jasper uses AI to create high-quality, SEO-optimized content quickly. It's especially helpful for scaling

content creation without sacrificing quality.
Website

- **Copy.ai**

Use for: Writing blog posts, product descriptions, ad copy, and social media content.

Why it's useful: Copy.ai is a versatile AI-powered tool that helps with creating copy in various formats. It offers templates for everything from landing pages to email newsletters.
Website

- **Writesonic**

Use for: Writing articles, blog posts, product descriptions, and social media posts.

Why it's useful: Writesonic uses AI to create SEO-optimized content in seconds. It can help scale content production and generate optimized material for a variety of use cases.
Website

- **INK   Editor**

Use for: SEO content writing and optimization.

Why it's useful: INK combines AI and SEO knowledge to help create content that is both engaging and optimized for search engines. It offers real-time SEO suggestions for   better   ranking.
Website

3. Analytics and Performance Tracking Platforms

These tools use AI to analyze and optimize SEO performance, track keyword rankings, and gather user behavior insights.

- **Google Analytics with AI Insights**
Use for: Tracking user behavior, traffic sources, and content performance.
Why it's useful: Google Analytics now offers AI-powered features such as automated insights, predictions, and anomaly detection to help track and optimize your website's performance.
Website

- **BrightEdge**
Use for: SEO performance tracking, keyword tracking, and competitive intelligence.
Why it's useful: BrightEdge uses AI to provide actionable insights into SEO performance and trends. It helps track keyword rankings, monitor traffic, and generate reports.
Website

- **HubSpot Analytics**
Use for: Marketing analytics, conversion tracking, and lead generation.
Why it's useful: HubSpot uses AI to provide detailed analytics on inbound marketing

campaigns, offering insights that help refine SEO and content strategies. Website

- **Hotjar**

  Use for: Heatmaps, session recordings, and user behavior analysis.

  Why it's useful: Hotjar's AI-powered tools help you understand how users interact with your website, providing insights into user behavior and ways to improve engagement and conversions. Website

- **SpyFu**

  Use for: Competitive analysis and keyword research.

  Why it's useful: SpyFu helps you analyze your competitors' SEO strategies and identify high-value keywords, using AI to track and predict performance trends. Website

4. AI for Structured Data and Schema Markup

These tools automate the process of adding structured data and schema markup to your content, improving visibility in rich snippets and Zero-Click Searches.

- **Schema   Pro**
  Use for: Adding schema markup to WordPress   sites.
  Why it's useful: Schema Pro is an AI-powered tool that automates the process of adding structured data to your website, enhancing its visibility in search results and   improving   SEO.
  Website

- **Mermaid**
  Use for: Visualizing structured data for web pages.
  Why it's useful: Mermaid helps you create diagrams and flowcharts to visualize how your data should be structured, which aids in implementing schema markup for better SERP   performance.
  Website

---

5. AI-Driven Content Research & Idea Generation

These tools help generate content ideas and suggest topics that resonate with your audience based on current trends and search queries.

- **AnswerThePublic**
  Use for: Generating content ideas based on search   queries.

Why it's useful: AnswerThePublic uses AI to provide a list of search queries and topics based on user input, helping you create content that meets search intent. Website

- **BuzzSumo**

  Use for: Content research and idea generation.

  Why it's useful: BuzzSumo uses AI to identify trending topics, top-performing content, and potential opportunities for link-building and guest posting. Website

---

6. AI for SEO Audits and Technical SEO

These tools help you analyze and audit your website's technical SEO performance, ensuring it's optimized for both search engines and users.

- **Screaming   Frog**

  Use for: Website crawling and SEO audits.

  Why it's useful: Screaming Frog is a powerful SEO tool that crawls your website and identifies technical SEO issues, such as broken links, missing meta descriptions, and poor redirects. Website

- **Sitebulb**

  Use for: SEO auditing and technical analysis.

  Why it's useful: Sitebulb's AI-driven audit reports provide actionable insights for fixing on-site SEO issues, from page speed to internal linking and accessibility.
  Website

Table of Contents :

www.ingramcontent.com/pod-product-compliance
Lightning Source LLC
Chambersburg PA
CBHW071010050326
40689CB00014B/3562